SCHIRMER'S LIB. OF MUSICAL CLASSICS

SERGEI RACHMANINOFF

Concertos

For the Piano

The Orchestra Accompaniments
Arranged for a Second Piano

FIRST CONCERTO
Op. 1
Library Vol. 1655

SECOND CONCERTO
Op. 18
Library Vol. 1576

THIRD CONCERTO
Op. 30
Library Vol. 1610

ISBN 978-0-7935-0500-5

G. SCHIRMER, Inc.

DISTRIBUTED BY

HAL•LEONARD®
CORPORATION
7777 W. BLUEMOUND RD. P.O. BOX 13819 MILWAUKEE, WI 53213

à Monsieur N. Dahl

Second Concerto

I

Sergei Rachmaninoff, Op. 18

Un poco più mosso.

Un poco più mosso.

accel.

accel.

II

III

Allegro scherzando. (Moto primo.) ($\flat$ = 116.)

Allegro scherzando. (Moto primo.) ($\flat$ = 116.)

Allegro scherzando. (Moto primo.) $(\quad=\quad)$ $(\quad=116.)$

38 **Allegro scherzando. (Moto primo.)** $(\quad=\quad)$ $(\quad=116.)$